Green Beans & Tambourines
Over 30 Summer Projects & Activities
for Fun-Loving Kids

Jennifer Storey Gillis
Illustrations by Patti Delmonte

A *Storey Publishing Book*

Storey Communications, Inc.

Green Beans & Tambourines

*The mission of Storey Communications is to serve our customers
by publishing practical information that encourages personal independence
in harmony with the environment.*

Edited by Amanda R. Haar
Cover design by Meredith Maker
Text design by Wanda Harper Joyce
Text production by Carol Jessop, Black Trout Design

Printed in Canada by Interglobe
Second Printing, November 1995

Some recipes and ideas in this book are adapted from
recipes in other books from Storey Communications, Inc.:
pages 2 and 9 from *Let's Grow!*, by Linda Tilgner; page 16
(Raspberry-Yogurt Shake) from *It's the Berries!*, by Liz
Anton and Beth Dooley; page 16 (Lemonade Slush) from
Surprising Citrus, by Audra and Jack Hendrickson; page 24
from *Pickles & Relishes*, by Andrea Chesman.

**Other books in this series by Jennifer Storey Gillis
and illustrated by Patti Delmonte**
In a Pumpkin Shell
An Apple a Day!
Hearts and Crafts

Library of Congress Cataloging-in-Publication Data

Gillis, Jennifer Storey. 1967–
    Green beans and tambourines : over 30 summer projects
& activities for fun-loving kids / Jennifer Storey Gillis :
illustrations by Patti Delmonte.
      p.   cm.
    "A Storey Publishing Book."
    ISBN 0-88266-893-5 (pbk.) : $9.95
    1. Amusements — Juvenile literature. 2. Recreation —
Juvenile literature. 3. Lesiure — Juvenile literature. [1.
Amusements.] I. Delmonte, Patti. II. Title. III. Title:
Green Beans and Tambourines.
GV182.9.G55 1995
793' .01922 — dc20   94-45733
                                        CIP
                                        AC

Table of Contents

Great Gardening Projects

Summer is the time of the year when the days are long, the sun is hot, and the garden does almost all of its growing. With a little spring planning, you can have flowers and vegetables beginning to sprout by the time you get out of school! It's amazing what you can produce with a handful of soil, some sunshine, water, and a little patience. Read on to learn how to grow some unusual (and kid-sized) gardens!

Teepee Bean Poles

Not only is this a great way to grow your beans, but once they have grown up the poles, you will have a wonderfully shady summer hiding place!

·· WHAT YOU WILL NEED ·· ·

- Large circle of garden space (about 6 feet across)
- Spade
- Rake
- 6 poles, 6–8 feet long
- Heavy twine
- String and scissors
- Pole bean seeds
- Water
- Hay
- Grown-up helper

1. Get your garden area ready by pulling up any weeds, turning the soil over with a spade, and adding fertilizer. Use your rake to smooth it.

2. You will need your grown-up helper for the next part. Stand your poles up in a circle in the garden plot. Bring the tops together to form a teepee. Tie the twine around the tops of the poles until they are secure. Push the bottom end of each pole down into the prepared soil so that the teepee stands on its own.

3. Put a thick layer of hay down inside of the teepee. This will keep weeds from growing in your hiding place.

4. Tie the twine to the bottom of one pole. Pull it tight and wrap it around the pole next to it, about one foot higher than your original tying spot.

Wrap it around the second pole twice, being sure to pull it tight, and then wrap it back around your original pole, about one foot higher than the spot you just came from. Keep zig-zagging up the two poles until you reach the top. Then wrap the twine around the pole you're on twice and pull it *straight across* to the other pole. Now zig-zag *down* the poles so that the twine forms little **x**-es between the poles. When you reach the bottom, cut and tie the string off to either pole.

5. You will need to zig-zag the twine up and down between all the poles except between the two poles that form the door to your teepee. Be patient. All that zigging and zagging takes time but it will give your green beans a great place to grow.

6. Use your finger to poke 6 holes about 1 inch deep around the base of each pole. Put one bean seed in each hole, cover it with soil, water it well, and let nature take its course!

7. The beans should sprout in a week to ten days. As they begin to come up, guide them gently to the poles and string. Soon, they will begin to climb on their own!

8. Pull out weeds that get in the way of the beans. Give the beans plenty of water and watch them grow. Be sure to touch the bean plants only when they are dry.

9. When the beans are ready, pick and eat!

Tire Garden

This is a good beginning for any kind of garden you want — a place for you to call your own! Take good care of it and you will see plenty of exciting results.

• • WHAT YOU WILL NEED • •

- Old car tire
- Good topsoil (enough to fill the tire completely)
- Water
- Seeds
- Strong hands for weeding
- Plenty of sunshine
- Grown-up helper

1 Put the tire on the grass in a spot that gets plenty of sunshine. Make sure you check with your grown-up helper before you decide on a spot. You want to be sure someone else doesn't have other plans for that same space.

2 Fill the tire with topsoil all the way to the top. Pack it firmly into all the spaces in the tire, but not so hard as to squeeze all the air out. This is where the growing will take place.

3 Using your finger, poke small holes in the soil for your seeds. Follow the seed packet instructions on how deep and how far apart to plant your seeds. Don't crowd them. Plants need room to grow. Drop your seeds in the holes and cover firmly with soil.

4 Water enough to make the soil damp, but do not drown your little seeds! Keep your eye on your garden and the weather. When it doesn't get enough natural watering from rain, you'll need to water it yourself.

5 Pull out any weeds as they grow up,

being careful not to disturb the plants.

6 With plenty of patience and care from you, and sunshine and water from nature, your plants should be sprouting in no time!

Rainbow Flower Garden

*All varieties of flowers and plants are beautiful and have their own special colors.
Try planting these kinds of flowers and plants together and see if you create
a rainbow of your own!*

··WHAT YOU WILL NEED··

- Corner of the family garden
- Trowel
- Rake
- Compost or fertilizer
- Water
- Seedlings (young plants) including red geraniums, orange marigolds, yellow zinnias, green ferns, blue petunias, and purple ageratum
- Sunshine

can usually plant your garden in early spring, depending on where you live.

 Work with your grown-up helper to choose a sunny corner of the garden where you can plant. Make sure you add some fertilizer or compost to the earth before raking it smooth.

 Using your trowel or your hand, dig little holes big enough for your plants. The holes should be about 6 inches apart and ½-inch deeper than the pots your seedlings are in. Gently remove your seedlings

Wait until the chance of frost has passed and the soil is warm. You

from their pots. Don't yank them —
you want their roots to stay intact.
Place your seedlings into the holes and
pat the soil around them firmly. They
should sit at just the same level in the
garden as they grew in their pots.

 Water your plants
often! They shouldn't
sit in a pool of water,
but they should never be dry either.

 Wait for your plants to
grow and blossom!
Invite your friends
over to see the rainbow you grew
yourself!

Garden Ideas

There's no end to the kinds of
gardens you can grow. Why not
try one of these:

◆ A butterfly garden filled with
nectar-rich flowers that
butterflies can't resist. Butterflies
are especially fond of daisies,
honeysuckle, and bee balm.

◆ A "favorite-color" garden
with plants that bloom in your
favorite color. If you like red,
plant red geraniums. If you're
partial to blue, try violets. Pink
fanciers will have a lot of fun
with impatiens.

◆ An Italian garden that will
grow wonderful treats to eat all
summer long (see page 10–11 for
instructions).

A Pickle Patch

Growing cucumbers for pickling is easy. All it takes is a few cucumber seeds, a little elbow grease, and a lot of room!

• • • WHAT YOU WILL NEED • • •

▸ Sunny spot in the garden (about 12 square feet per plant)
▸ Spade
▸ Rake
▸ Water
▸ Cucumber seeds

 When the chance of frost has passed, use your spade to turn over the soil in your garden, adding some compost as you go.

 Rake the soil smooth. Gently push your cucumber seeds into the soil. Seeds should be planted about 1 inch deep and at least 2 feet apart. Cucumbers really like to spread out!

 Cover the seeds with soil, and water well.

 In about 14 days the cucumber vines will begin to poke up out of the soil. Now just stand back and watch them spread!

See pages 24–25 for an easy No-Cook Pickles recipe.

Grow a Bottled Cucumber

You can "magically" grow a cucumber in a bottle and
keep all your friends guessing how you did it!

·· WHAT YOU WILL NEED ·· ·

▸ Narrow-necked bottle
▸ Newspaper
▸ Knife
▸ Grown-up helper

1. Find a baby cucumber that has begun to grow on the vine. It needs to be small enough so that it will fit inside the neck of the bottle.

2. Gently slide it inside the bottle *without* breaking it off its stem! Try to find a young cucumber that is shaded by lots of leaves, but if that isn't possible, try to shade it with newspapers.

3. Stand back and watch it grow! It should fill the bottle as it gets bigger, but be sure to have your grown-up helper help you cut it off the vine before it gets too big.

4. Have fun watching your friends try to figure out how the cucumber got in there!

Italian Garden

It's fun and easy to grow an Italian garden. Planting just a few different ingredients can help you create lots of Italian foods. Try the Italian Garden Tomato Salad on page 21 and let your imagination go from there!

··WHAT YOU WILL NEED··

- Sunny corner of the garden
- Water
- Spade
- Rake
- Trowel
- Fertilizer
- Basil, tomato, and onion seedlings from a garden store or nursery

 Mix some fertilizer in your soil and rake it smooth before you begin planting.

 Dig little holes for each plant. The plants should be about 5 inches apart. Put each plant in a hole and push the soil around it firmly. The plants should sit at just the same level in the garden as they grew in their pots. You should plant all the basil together, all the onions together, and all the tomatoes together.

 Water the plants often, never letting them get too dry.

4 Wait and watch as your plants grow. Remember to

◆ Plant your onions in early spring, but wait until the warmer weather to put in your basil and tomato plants.

◆ Use compact tomato plants for best results. Plants named 'Pixie' or 'Tiny Tim' are good choices.

◆ Your tomato plants will need some support while growing. (All those tomatoes can be heavy!) Put a tomato cage around your young plants or insert a stake in the soil directly next to each plant.

pull any weeds that pop up. Be patient and your hard work will pay off!

See pages 21–22 for a delicious Italian Garden Tomato Salad recipe.

Garden Toad House

Toads love to gobble up harmful bugs and pests, so they can help keep your plants healthy and thriving all summer long. Best of all, toads are fairly easy to attract to your yard. Just provide the right kind of house and a swimming hole, and with some luck, you may have a new neighbor soon!

·· WHAT YOU WILL NEED ··

- 2 plastic butter or cottage cheese containers at least 3 inches deep
- Handful of pebbles
- Scissors

Cut a doorway about 1-½ inches high and 2 inches wide from the edge of one of your containers.

 Place this container upside down in a shady spot near the edge of your garden and place the pebbles on top. The weight of the pebbles will keep your house from blowing away on windy days.

 Dig a hole near your new Toad House deep enough and wide enough to hold your other container right-side-up. If your hole's a little too big, fill in the edges with loose dirt.

 Fill the second container with water. This will be your toad's swimming hole.

◆ You can also make a toad house from a chipped flower pot or bowl. Just make sure the doorway is big enough for a toad to fit through and ask a grown-up to help you place it in your yard.

◆ Decorate your toad house using waterproof markers. Add windows, a chimney, flowerboxes — whatever you think will make your toad feel at home.

 Sit back and wait for a toad to discover the wonderful home you created. Be patient. It may take several weeks for a toad to find your yard.

Scrumptious Summertime Recipes

Summertime recipes are different from recipes for any other time of the year. Some are fresh from the garden, others are cool and refreshing, and others are for a barbeque. But they all have one thing in common: They are fun to make and even more fun to eat! Share your creations with family and friends. They won't believe what you made with your own two hands!

Delicious Drinks

If hot summer weather leaves you longing for a cool drink, these recipes are for you!

Minty Sun Tea

··WHAT YOU WILL NEED···

- Large glass pitcher
- 5–6 mint tea bags (any kind you like)
- Cold water
- Glasses
- Ice
- Lemon and honey

1. Put the tea bags in the pitcher and then fill it up with cold water.

2. Cover the top of the pitcher with plastic wrap and put on a sunny window or outside in the direct sunlight. Let the tea "brew" for an hour or two then check to see how it's doing. It should be tea color now!

3. Serve in a glass with plenty of ice and add lemon — or honey if you like sweet tea. Top with a sprig of mint and serve.

Be sure to put the pitcher in a safe place if you make the tea outside. Cats and dogs love to know what's going on and they may accidentally knock it over!

15

Lemonade Slush

Serves 4

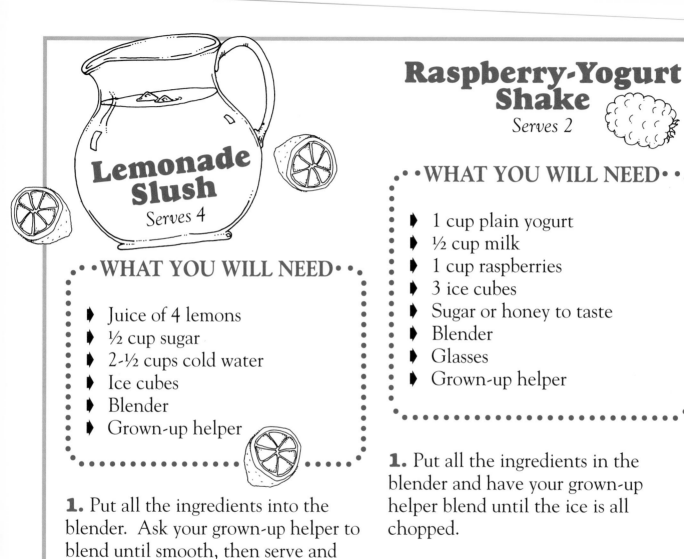

- ▶ Juice of 4 lemons
- ▶ ½ cup sugar
- ▶ 2-½ cups cold water
- ▶ Ice cubes
- ▶ Blender
- ▶ Grown-up helper

1. Put all the ingredients into the blender. Ask your grown-up helper to blend until smooth, then serve and drink. This will make enough for you and three friends.

Raspberry-Yogurt Shake

Serves 2

- ▶ 1 cup plain yogurt
- ▶ ½ cup milk
- ▶ 1 cup raspberries
- ▶ 3 ice cubes
- ▶ Sugar or honey to taste
- ▶ Blender
- ▶ Glasses
- ▶ Grown-up helper

1. Put all the ingredients in the blender and have your grown-up helper blend until the ice is all chopped.

2. Pour into two glasses and drink with a friend.

16

Backyard Barbeque

*Whether you try these recipes
for lunch or dinner,
you'll be a hero to your
hungry friends!*

Buttered Barbeque Corn

··WHAT YOU WILL NEED··

- 1 ear of corn for each person
- 1 paper bag
- 1 tablespoon butter for each ear of corn
- Aluminum foil
- Salt and pepper
- Grill
- Grown-up helper

1 Shuck each ear of corn and put the husks in a paper bag for now. (You can add them to the compost pile later while your corn is cooking!) Rinse the ears and let them dry for a few minutes. Put each ear on a piece of aluminum foil — about 3 inches longer than the corn.

2 Put the butter on the corn and sprinkle it with salt and pepper. Wrap each ear up

Be very careful when you unwrap your corn! It will be very hot and steamy. You may need some grown-up help to get it on the table.

HOT STUFF!

tightly and take the silver bundles out to your grilling grown-up.

3 Have your grown-up helper put the ears on the grill and turn them every few minutes or so. The corn should cook about 20 minutes. When the corn is done, carefully unwrap each ear and serve with burgers and the rest of your barbeque feast!

Buried Treasure Burgers

WHAT YOU WILL NEED

- 1 pound of lean hamburger meat
- Egg
- Bowl for mixing
- Buried Treasure filling of your choice — try sliced or shredded cheese, onion, tomato, pickle, bacon, or olives
- Clean hands for making the patties
- Plate for holding the finished patties
- Spatula
- Grill
- Grown-up helper

1 Put the hamburger into your bowl and crack the egg into it. Using your clean hands, mix the egg and hamburger together well.

 2 Divide the hamburger into 8 equal-sized portions and flatten into big circles about ½-inch thick.

 3 Place your buried treasure in the center of 4 of your patties. You don't have to put the same treasure in each burger. Mix them up for a fun surprise.

4 Place the patties without treasures on top of the patties with treasures and pinch the edges tightly shut.

 5 Put the patties on a plate and tell your grown-up helper they are

ready for the grill. Wash your hands after you finish making the patties. Cook about 6 minutes on each side or until the burgers are cooked through.

 6 Watch the surprise on everyone's face when they discover the buried treasure!

Banana Boats

··WHAT YOU WILL NEED··

- 1 banana for each person
- Aluminum foil
- Mini-marshmallows
- Chocolate chips
- Spoons for eating
- Oven mitt
- Grill
- Grown-up helper

1 Peel back one strip of the banana peel, being careful not to remove it altogether. Using a small spoon, take 4 scoops out of the banana. You can eat the scoops now or save them for a snack later.

2 Fill the hollow place in the banana with chocolate chips and marshmallows. Put the peel back in place and wrap the entire banana tightly with aluminum foil.

3 Have your grown-up helper put the banana boats onto the grill. Cook for about 20 minutes.

4 Have your helper take the boats off the grill with an oven mitt. Carefully unwrap the foil and let cool — as the filling will be very hot! Dig in and enjoy every bite of your boat!

20

Goodies from Your Garden

You worked so hard to plant and grow your garden.
Now here's something to do with your harvest!

Italian Garden Tomato Salad

• • WHAT YOU WILL NEED • •

- 3–4 large red tomatoes from your Italian Garden
- ½ pound fresh mozzarella cheese
- 10 clean, dry basil leaves from your Italian Garden
- Olive oil
- Balsamic vinegar
- Plate
- Knife
- Cookie cutter
- Black pepper
- Grown-up helper

 1 Get your grown-up helper to slice your tomatoes and cheese for you. You can then cut the cheese into small circles using the cookie cutter. Use a cutter that will make circles that are about the same size as your tomato slices. If you don't have a cookie cutter, try using the neck of a baby food jar — washed, of course!

 2 Arrange the cheese and tomatoes on the plate, switching back and forth from tomato to cheese, tomato to cheese, so that every tomato slice is topped with a piece of cheese.

3 Put the basil leaves on top of each stack of tomato and cheese, then carefully drizzle a little oil and balsamic vinegar over everything. Grind a little black pepper on top. *Buon apetito!*

Teepee Bean Salad

•••WHAT YOU WILL NEED•••

- A big bowlful of beans from your Teepee Bean Garden
- Onion
- Knife
- Bowl
- 1 tablespoon olive oil
- 1 tablespoon red or white vinegar
- Salt and pepper
- Lemon juice
- Grown-up helper

1. Wash the beans and snap the ends off.

2. Have a grown-up helper slice the onion into small pieces and put the slices in a bowl with the beans.

3. Sprinkle the beans with 1 teaspoon of lemon juice and 1 tablespoon each of oil and vinegar. Mix well. Add salt and pepper if you like.

4. Put beans in the refrigerator and eat them cold — a perfect side dish for any summer meal!

23

No-Cook Pickles

WHAT YOU WILL NEED

- 6 cups thinly sliced cucumbers
- 1 cup thinly sliced onions
- 2 teaspoons pickling salt
- 1 teaspoon celery seeds
- 2 cups white sugar
- 1 cup white vinegar

- 3 cups water
- 2 clean one-quart jars with plastic lids (no metal)
- Large mixing bowl
- Spoon
- Grown-up helper

 1 Wash the jars carefully in hot soapy water, then rinse and dry them well.

 2 While your grown-up helper is slicing up the cucumbers and onions, you can begin mixing all the other ingredients together in a bowl.

 3 Add the cucumbers and onions to the vinegar mixture and stir it carefully so that everything is mixed well.

 4 Let the pickles sit and rest for about 3 hours. Then, work with your helper to put the pickles into jars. Fill each jar almost to the top with pickles and screw the lids on tight. Store pickles in the refrigerator.

These pickles will last up to 6 months as long as they stay cool in the refrigerator. Be sure to label and date each jar. If you give these as a gift to someone, make sure to tell them that they need to be stored in the fridge. Enjoy!

Frozen Treats

*Everyone knows that one of the best things about
the summer is ice cream and ice pops.
Here's a way to have the best ice cream
and popsicles of all — the kind you make yourself!*

Homemade Ice Cream
Serves 6

*Here's a fun and easy way to make ice cream yourself. This recipe is for basic vanilla
but you can add your favorite fruit, chocolate or carob chips, granola, or other goodies
to create your favorite flavor.*

• • • • • • • • • • • WHAT YOU WILL NEED • • • • • • • • • • •

- 1 quart heavy or light cream
- ¾ cup of sugar or ⅓ cup of honey
- 1 tablespoon vanilla extract
- 9-inch x 13-inch baking pan
- Large metal mixing bowl

- Cleaned flat space in your freezer large enough to hold baking pan
- Electric mixer or rotary egg beater
- Plastic wrap
- Grown-up helper

Turn your freezer to the coldest setting possible.

 Combine the cream, sugar or honey, and vanilla in the mixing bowl. Stir thoroughly.

 Pour mixture into the baking pan. Place pan in the freezer and let chill for 30 minutes to 1 hour, or until the mixture is mushy but not solid.

 While your mixture's chilling, wash and dry your bowl and put it in the refrigerator. You'll need it to be good and chilly in the next step.

 Remove the pan from the freezer and your chilled bowl from the refrigerator. Scrape the ice cream mixture from the pan into the chilled bowl. Ask your grown-up helper to mix the ice cream with the electric mixer or egg beater until smooth.

 Pour the ice cream back into the pan and return to freezer. Wash and dry your bowl again and put it in the refrigerator.

continued…

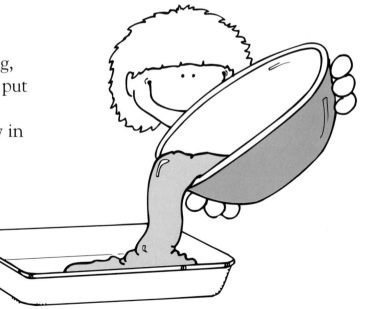

27

When almost solid again, repeat the scraping and mixing process. If you want to add fruit or nuts stir them in after your grown-up helper has finished beating the ice cream the second time. Pour the ice cream back into the pan, cover with plastic wrap, and freeze until solid. (Now you can wash, dry, and put your bowl away!)

Invite a few friends over and have an ice cream party! (See the next page for ideas on how to throw a Super Summer Sundae Fest.)

Super Summer Sundaes

This is a great dessert to share with friends. Put the toppings into a row of bowls and let everyone create their own masterpiece in a sundae assembly line!

··•WHAT YOU WILL NEED··•

- Your favorite flavor(s) of ice cream or frozen yogurt
- Ice cream scoop or spoon
- Large bowls for the sundaes
- Any combination of the following items, and any others you can think of: hot fudge or butterscotch sauce, fresh fruit, granola, nuts, raisins, chocolate chips, crumbled cookies, crumbled candy bars, chocolate milk powder, whipped cream
- Hearty appetite!

1 Put two scoops of ice cream or yogurt into each bowl.

2 Now the fun begins! Decorate the ice cream with any of the toppings you like best. While it might be fun to pile everything on, try mixing 1 or 2 toppings at a time and then taste your creation — if you add too many at once, you might not want to eat it! Remember, a little goes a long way, so don't use too much of any one topping.

Zebra Pops

Serves 12

Here's a way to combine some of your favorite fruit juice flavors into a pop that's as fun to look at as it is to eat!

······· **WHAT YOU WILL NEED** ·······

- ▶ 12 clear plastic cups (6-ounce)
- ▶ 24 ounces each of 3 of your favorite flavored fruit juices
- ▶ 12 wooden craft sticks
- ▶ 12 squares of plastic wrap large enough to cover the top of each cup

- ▶ 12 rubber bands
- ▶ Freezable tray or cookie sheet
- ▶ Clear space in freezer large enough to accommodate your tray

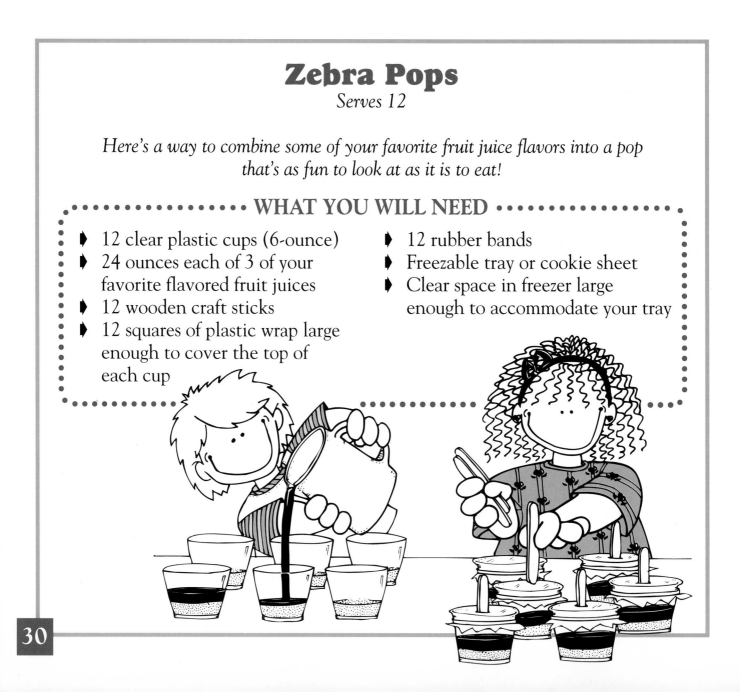

Arrange your cups on the tray. Pour about 1 inch of fruit juice into each cup and place entire tray in freezer for 20 minutes or until frozen.

 Remove tray from freezer and pour 1 inch of another flavor juice into each cup.

 Place one square of plastic wrap over the top of each cup and secure with a rubber band to form a lid.

 Poke 1 craft stick through the center of each plastic wrap lid.

 Return entire tray to freezer for another 20 minutes or until the second layer of juice is frozen.

 Remove the tray from the freezer and remove the rubber

Tips for Terrific Zebra Pops

◆ Zebra Pops look best when you use 2 or 3 different colored fruit juice.

◆ Try adding a layer of your favorite flavored yogurt to your Pop for an extra-creamy, white-striped treat.

bands and plastic wrap. Your popsicle sticks should be frozen into place by now. Pour 1 inch of the third flavor of juice into each cup and freeze for a final 20 minutes.

 To remove Zebra Pops from cups, gently roll them back and forth in your hands (stick side up) until loose. Enjoy!

31

Pack a Perfect Picnic!

Whether you head to the beach, the park, the lake, the mountains, the pool, or just the backyard, a picnic is a perfect thing to do on a warm summer day. These recipes are so good you may not be able to wait until summer!

Perfect Summer Picnic Menu

Fresh fruit
Minty Sun Tea or Lemonade Slush,
pages 15–16
Peanut Butter Pies, page 33
Creepy-Crawly Fruit Critters, page 34

Peanut Butter Pies

Serves 4

Peanut Butter Pies are a great picnic treat because you can make them on the spot.
So pack up your peanut butter and favorite toppings and get ready to create a
Peanut Butter Pie!

• • WHAT YOU WILL NEED • • •

- ▶ 4 rice cakes or English muffin halves
- ▶ Plastic jar or tub of peanut butter (as much as you think you'll need for 4 pies)
- ▶ Your favorite peanut butter topping — try raisins, banana slices, carrot sticks, or apple wedges
- ▶ Spreader
- ▶ Enough plastic containers or bags to get all your toppings to your picnic site

1. Using your spreader, spread a layer of peanut butter onto your rice cake or English muffin half.

2. Use your favorite toppings to decorate the top of your pie. Make a silly face with raisins and banana slices. Write your initials with carrot sticks.

3. Admire your artwork and then eat it right up.

Creepy-Crawly Fruit Critters

1. Spear 1 grape with a toothpick and slide the grape to the middle of the toothpick.

2. Add the other grapes to the ends of the toothpick.

3. Insert another toothpick through the center of the middle grape so it forms a cross with the first toothpick.

4. Insert the last toothpick through the grape on either end of your ant to again form a cross with the first toothpick.

5. Don't panic! These ants won't spoil any of your picnic fun.

1. Ask your grown-up helper to slice your apple into four equal pieces. Ask him or her to cut out the core and seeds.

2. Insert 1 toothpick into one tip of each apple slice.

3. Carefully slide your grape onto the ends of the toothpicks to give your Ladybug a head.

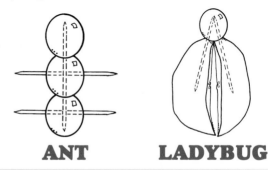

ANT **LADYBUG**

Picnic Packer's Puzzle

Going on a picnic takes some planning and a lot of packing. Here's a fun little puzzle to help remind you of some of the most important things to take.

ACROSS

1. Remember the _____ to hold your drinks.
3. You'll need a big picnic _____ to carry all your food.
5. Don't forget the _____ to wipe your hands.
6. Every good picnic packer takes along an extra _____ to take their garbage home in.

DOWN

2. Whether they're made of paper or plastic, you'll need a stack of _____ to eat off of.
3. Take along a _____ to spread your picnic out on.
4. Bring a big _____ so you can enjoy all your picnic treats!

Summer Fun and Games

During the summer the weather is warmer, the days are longer, and there is plenty of time for fun and games. Whether you are riding in the car, going to the beach, or just looking for something of your own to celebrate, these games and projects will fill every day with fun.

Are We There Yet?

These games are great if you are riding in the car, lying on the beach, dipping your toes in the pool, or just looking for something to do. Some of the games are designed to be played alone, so all you need to bring is your brain!

Alphabet

1. Choose a category like "vegetables" or "breakfast cereals."

2. Take turns thinking of something that fits in the category that starts with the next letter of the alphabet. For example, if the category is "vegetables," the first player might say, "**A**rtichoke," the next player might say, "**B**eans," and the next player might say, "**C**arrots."

3. If you can't think of anything when it is your turn, you get a point. The person with the fewest points at the end of the game wins.

License Plates

1. Before you take a car trip, make a list of the fifty states and get your grown-up helper to make a copy for all the people going on the trip. (You might want to make some extras to keep in the glove compartment for other long car rides.)

2. Give a list to everyone in the car who is playing. Look out the window at the license plates of the cars and trucks going by.

3. Use a pencil to put a check next to every state you see a license plate from.

4. The winner is the person who has the most checks at the end of the ride!

"I Went on a Camping Trip…"

1. This is a memory game. The first player says, "I went on a camping trip and I brought a flashlight" (or any object that you would take camping).

2. The next player says, "I went on a camping trip and I brought a flashlight and a sleeping bag."

3. The next player says, "I went on a camping trip and I brought a flashlight, a sleeping bag, and a tent." Before you can add your own item you must remember what everyone else has said first! The person who remembers the longest list wins!

Rain, Rain, Go Away

Even in the summer there are days you have to stay inside. When you find yourself looking out the window at puddles and rain, put your mind to work.

◆ Read a book.

◆ Write a letter, a poem, or a song.

◆ Say the alphabet backwards.

◆ Read A.A. Milne's poem *"Waiting at the Window"* about two rain drops, John and James. Look for it in his book *Now We Are Six*.

Or try your hand at these projects and see if you can make the sun shine inside!

Rainy Day Postcards

•••WHAT YOU WILL NEED•••

- Construction paper
- Scissors
- White paper
- Glue
- Markers or crayons
- Postcard stamp
- Black pen
- Ruler

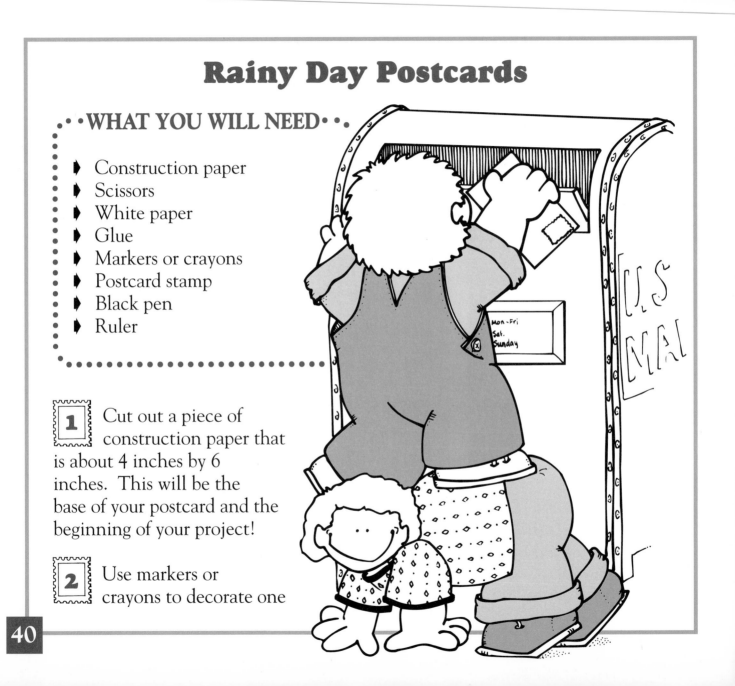

1 Cut out a piece of construction paper that is about 4 inches by 6 inches. This will be the base of your postcard and the beginning of your project!

2 Use markers or crayons to decorate one

40

side of your postcard, or use small pieces of colored construction paper to make a collage picture. Draw places you have been, places you'd like to go, or things you have done this summer!

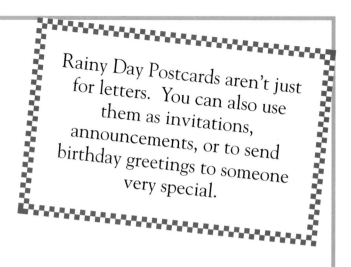

Rainy Day Postcards aren't just for letters. You can also use them as invitations, announcements, or to send birthday greetings to someone very special.

3 Cut a piece of white paper exactly the same size as the postcard. Carefully glue it to the back of your postcard (the side without the picture) and let it dry before you go on to the next step.

4 When your postcard is dry, use your black pen to write on the white side. Neatly draw a line down the middle (from top to bottom) of the postcard. Then draw four lines on the right side of the postcard. These four lines should be in the middle of the right side. They are for the address of the person you are sending the postcard to. At the very top of the left side of the postcard, write what

your postcard is a picture of. The rest of that side is for your note.

5 Save your postcards for another day or write and send them immediately! Grandmas and grandpas always love to hear what's going on. It would also be nice to send a postcard to your friend at camp or to your favorite teacher!

6 Whatever you do, don't forget to put a stamp on your postcard before you mail it.

Egghead Planters

These goofy little planters are fun to make and even more fun to watch as they grow.

· · WHAT YOU WILL NEED · ·

- Raw egg in shell
- Waterproof felt tip markers
- Potting soil
- Grass or bean sprout seeds
- Egg carton

2 Carefully rinse out the inside of the egg and then dry the inside and outside with a paper towel. Handle the egg shell *very* carefully, so you don't break it!

1 Over the kitchen sink, carefully tap the top off of your egg and pour out the egg yolk and white. If you can use the raw egg in a recipe within the next 24 hours, pour it into a small bowl, cover with plastic wrap, and refrigerate until ready to use.

3 Using your markers, draw a silly face on your Egghead. Give it eyes, lips, a nose, ears, even glasses!

 4 Place your Egghead in the egg carton and carefully fill him (or her!) up with soil, leaving about ¼-inch of room from the top.

5 Sprinkle the soil with grass seed.

 6 Cover the seeds with a light coating of soil, and water until damp but not soaking wet.

 7 Keep your Egghead in a warm dark place for one week. Check the soil during the week to make sure it stays moist.

 8 As soon as you see hair starting to sprout, move your Egghead to a sunny windowsill where you can watch its hair grow in.

"Eggs-perimint" with Your Egghead

You can change the kind and color of your Egghead's hair just by using different seeds. Grass seed will grow straight green hair. Sprout seeds will grow in curly and white. "Eggs-periment" with your Egghead and see how silly it can get!

A Day at the Beach

The beach is a marvelous place to play and have fun. As long as you are careful in the sun and the water, your day will be a winner!

The Shell Game

•••WHAT YOU WILL NEED•••

▶ Large shells for digging and tossing
▶ Stick
▶ Fun-loving playmate

1. Find a place on the beach where the sand is packed firmly.

2. Use a large shell to dig a small hole, about three times larger than the size of the shell.

3. Walk in a straight line about 10 steps away from the first hole and dig a second hole about the same size as the first.

4. Using your stick, draw two rings around each hole. Then label the inside circle "5" and the outside circle "1."

5. Each player gets three large shells. Standing behind one of the holes, players try to toss their shells into the other hole. The object is to get your shell(s) into the hole — that will earn you 10 points! If a shell lands in the inside circle you get 5 points. If a shell lands in the outside circle you get 1 point. If the other player's shell bumps your shell out of a good position or into a better position, your shell stays where it lands!

6. Keep score and have fun! The game is over when somebody wins, somebody gets too hot, or the waves wash your board away!

Seaside Plaster Casting

•••WHAT YOU WILL NEED•••

- Flat, sandy spot on the beach
- Plaster of Paris
- Measuring cup
- Clean coffee can
- Bucket
- Paint stirrer

1. Find a level spot on the beach away from the surf where the sand is moist but not packed hard.

2. Smooth the sand with your hand and then press, straight down into the sand with the palm of your hand or bottom of your foot. Don't press too deep but be sure to make a good impression.

3. Following the directions on the plaster of Paris package, measure the appropriate amount of plaster into the coffee can.

4. Fill your bucket with sea water. Use your measuring cup to measure the right amount of water into the coffee can.

5. Quickly mix the sea water and plaster. Pour it into your hand- or footprint. Be sure to pour your plaster as soon as it's mixed. If you're not quick enough, the plaster will harden right in the can!

You can make a plaster casting even if you're not at the beach. Just fill a disposable aluminum pie pan with moist sand. Smooth it over and make your print. Follow the same casting instructions listed here. Seaside plaster castings make great paper weights and perfect gifts for moms, dads, and grandparents!

6. Let your plaster casting dry for about 10 minutes or until it feels very hard to the touch.

7. Gently lift your plaster casting from the sand, and continue to let it dry print-side up for a few minutes. You can paint or decorate your casting later with acrylic paint.

47

What to Take to the Beach Word Search

Here's a fun word search to play on your way to the beach or while you're there. Use the clues to help you figure out what each of the hidden words might be and get searching!

1. You wear it on your head.

2. You put it on your skin to protect you from sunburn.

3. With a _____ and a _____ you can build sandcastles and dig for buried treasure.

4. One of these is great to fly on a windy day.

5. A pair of these will keep the sun out of your eyes.

6. You'd be very sorry if you forgot to wear this swimming-essential to the beach!

```
L O Z K M A S A S
H P U I M E H A U
A N T T R V O Y N
T O W E L M V E G
X O R G T U E P L
L A M T I R L O A
I N G P C H A T S
A Z T S I E R R S
P I N C Y N W E E
Q U P O N T L S S
S W I M S U I T E
```

Flag Day and Fourth of July Fun

If you're looking for yet another reason to celebrate this summer, mark your calendar for June 14, Flag Day, and July 4, the Fourth of July.

What Is Flag Day?

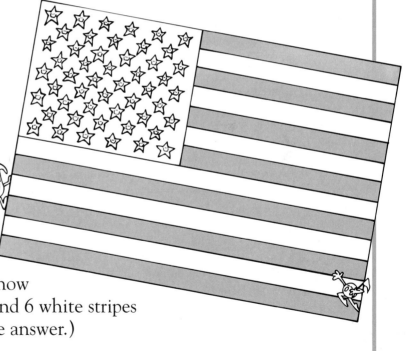

June 14th is known as Flag Day in the United States. It's the day we remember and celebrate when the Continental Congress adopted the first official flag of the United States! It looked a little different from the way our flag looks today. It had 13 stripes like the modern flag, but it had only 13 stars, for the original 13 colonies. Do you know what our 50 white stars and 7 red and 6 white stripes stand for now? (See page 60 for the answer.)

Make Your Own Flag

- Construction paper
- Scissors
- Ruler
- Glue
- Chopstick for flying your flag
- Hole punch
- String

50

◆ Make flags as party favors for a birthday party. Party guests can all have their own flags waiting for them at their seats!

◆ Look up "Flags" in an encyclopedia. Copy one of the beautiful designs you see.

1 Cut out a piece of construction paper that is about 4-½ inches by 6-½ inches. This will be the background color for your flag.

2 Using different colors of paper, cut out stars, stripes, animals...any shape that you would like on your flag! It might stand for something you like to do or it might just be a shape that's fun to make!

3 Arrange the shapes on your flag and glue them to the background. Make your flag as colorful and filled with designs as you'd like — remember, it's *your* flag.

4 Punch a hole at the top and bottom corners of one of the short ends of the flag. Cut two small pieces of string and lace one through each of the holes. Tie to the chopstick (or any other straight stick) that is your flag pole. Wave your flag proudly!

Flag Cake

- 1 box yellow or white cake mix
- Eggs, oil, or water (read the directions on the box to see exactly what you will need)
- Bowl
- 9-inch x 13-inch cake pan
- Sliced strawberries
- Blueberries that have been washed and drained
- White icing, enough for one cake
- Knife
- Grown-up helper

1 Follow the directions on the cake mix box for making the cake. Ask your grown-up helper to preheat the oven before you start, so you don't have to wait for it to heat up.

2 When the cake has been cooked and your grown-up helper has taken it out of the oven, let it cool for at least one hour.

3 Using your knife, ice the cake top with white icing. Try to get it smooth and even — this is the background of the American flag you are making!

4 Use the blueberries to create a field of stars in the top left corner. Make red strawberry "stripes" across the rest of the cake.

5 Take a picture of your cake before your family digs in — once they start, this flag won't wave for long!

Bicycles on Parade

What would the Fourth of July be without a parade? And what better kind of parade than a Bicycle Parade of you and your friends. Share these bicycle decorating ideas with your friends and form a parade of your own.

Ribbon Sparklers

- Newspaper
- 2 feet of red, white, or blue ribbon
- Small bowl
- Water
- Glue
- Paint brush
- Glitter
- Dowel or stick 6-inches long
- Thumbtack

1. Open up your newspaper on a large flat work surface.

2. Lay your ribbon out flat across the paper.

3. Using your paint brush, mix about 2 tablespoons of glue and 1 tablespoon of water in a small bowl.

4. Paint the glue and water mixture onto one side of your ribbon and sprinkle with as much glitter as you like. Let your ribbon dry for about 15 minutes and then turn over and repeat the painting and sprinkling process.

5. After the second side of your ribbon is dry, use your thumbtack to fasten it to the top of your dowel or stick. Fasten your Ribbon Sparkler to the grips of your bike for a dazzling effect.

Make a No-Motor Motor Bike

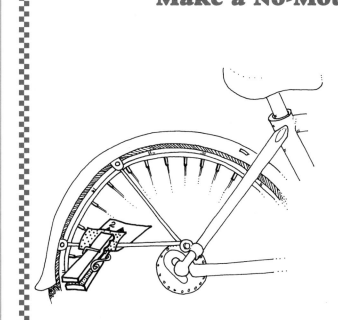

Your bike doesn't have a motor but you can make it sound like it does with just a clothespin and a playing card. Attach the clothespin to your bike's fender strut and insert a playing card into the clothespin. When your bike wheel turns, the spokes will hit the playing card and make a motor noise. Be sure you keep fingers far away from the spokes of your wheel whenever it is moving.

Patriotic Pinwheels

- 6-inch square piece of red, white, or blue construction paper
- Scissors
- Glue stick
- Pencil with eraser
- Thumbtack

1. Using your pencil, draw two lines to connect the opposite corners of your square of paper. The two lines should form a large **x** marking the center of your square.

2. From each corner, cut along the **x** lines to about ½ inch from the center of the square. Be sure *not* to cut all the way to the center! You should now have four floppy triangles all attached at the center.

3. Lay your paper in front of you and dab the left corner of the top triangle

Here are some other ways to make your bike more festive:

- Tie short red, white, and blue streamers to your handle bars.
- Tape a flag or pinwheel to the frame of your bike, just below your seat.
- Wrap red, white, and blue crepe paper around your bike frame and weave it between your spokes.

with your glue stick. Now bend and press that corner to the center of the square until the glue holds. Turn your paper ¼ turn and again dab and fold the left corner of the top triangle to the center. Continue turning, dabbing, and folding the square until all four corners are folded in.

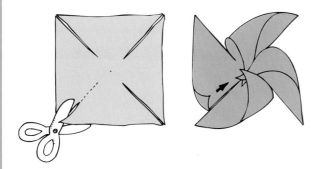

4. Lift your pinwheel up and position the center of the back against the eraser of your pencil. Press the thumbtack through the front center of the Pinwheel and into the eraser. Presto Pinwheel!

Ride Smart, Ride Safe

No matter where you're riding your bike, you should always wear your helmet. No one ever expects to fall off their bike but if you do, a helmet can protect you from serious injury. Plus, you can decorate your helmet with stickers and ribbons to match your bike. So be smart, be safe, and wear your helmet.

Ta-Ra-Da-Boom-De-Ay Tambourine and Other Noisemakers

Every parade needs a little music and a little noise. Here are some fun and easy instruments you can make and play yourself.

Comb-Kazoo

• • WHAT YOU WILL NEED • • •

- ▶ Ruler
- ▶ Clean plastic comb
- ▶ Scissors
- ▶ Wax paper
- ▶ Favorite tune

1. Measure the length and width of your comb.

2. Cut a piece of wax paper that's the same length and twice as wide as your comb.

3. Fold the paper around the comb so that the open edges of the paper meet on the toothy side of your comb.

4. Place the toothy side of the comb and open paper edges just inside your lips. Close your lips and hum. This may take a little practice and it will probably tickle your lips. So get ready to giggle and hum a happy tune.

Ta·Ra·Da·Boom·De·Ay Tambourine

1. Place your beans, corn, or pebbles in one of the pie plates.

2. Put the other pie plate on top of the first, bottom side up. Staple the edges of the pie plates together.

3. Staple your ribbons onto the edges of the plates and get ready to make some noise!

Answer Page

Picnic Packer's Puzzle

Page 35

ACROSS
1. CUPS
3. BASKET
5. NAPKINS
6. TRASHBAG

DOWN
2. PLATES
3. BLANKET
4. APPETITE

Star and Stripes Question

Page 49

Each of the 13 stripes represents one of the 13 original states. The 50 stars represent the current 50 states.

What to Take to the Beach Word Search

Page 48